ALAN STIVELL

COMPLETE RECORDINGS ILLUSTRATED

IAN BLENKINSOP
& ANDREW SPARKE

Essential Discographies No.39

APS Books,
4 Oakleigh Road, Stourbridge, West Midlands, DY8 2JX

APS Books is a subsidiary of the APS Publications imprint

www.andrewsparke.com

Copyright ©2021 Ian Blenkinsop and Andrew Sparke
All rights reserved.

Ian Blenkinsop and Andrew Sparke have asserted their right to be identified as the authors of this work in accordance with the Copyright Designs and Patents Act 1988

First published worldwide by APS Books in 2021

No part of this publication may be reproduced, stored in or introduced into a retrieval system, or transmitted, in any form, or by any means (electronic, mechanical, photocopying, recording or otherwise) without the written permission of the publisher except that brief selections may be quoted or copied without permission, provided that full credit is given.

ISBN 9781789960792

Photographs unless otherwise stated courtesy of Jérémy Kergoulay

NOTES

This short book simply collects the recorded work of the brilliant Celtic music revivalist Alan Stivell and its aim is to save record buyers hours of research online while providing a neat catalogue for the bookshelf.

COMPILER'S NOTE

The early seventies were an interesting time to find your musical identity. Eclecticism was more or less a given. To go and see Steeleye Span, Tangerine Dream and Jethro Tull in the space of a week (as I did in 1974) was not considered unusual. To pigeonhole yourself within a single genre was very much the exception. So it was unsurprising that I should come across a then obscure Celtic music revivalist called Alan Stivell, and that my interest would be piqued. Rooting around the local record store, I came across *Renaissance of the Celtic Harp*. I got the music from the opening chords of *Ys*. By the time I got to the extended tour of the Gaelic nations in Gaeltacht I was sold. What I didn't know then, as the album is primarily traditional, is the extent to which Stivell was developing a distinctive brand of Celtic folk-rock, a counterpart to what Fairport and Steeleye were doing for English folk music. So *À L'Olympia* came as a very welcome surprise. I didn't actually get to see him live until the July Wakes festival in 1976 at Park Hall near Chorley (later to be the site of the Camelot theme park). He didn't fail to impress.

What I also like about Stivell is that, in the course of a career spanning six decades, he has remained open to new ideas and inspiration from outside Celtic music. Brian Boru used sampling and drum loops, for example, and his collaboration with Youssou N'Dour on 1 Douar was a revelation. For me, at least, this is similar to Peter Gabriel, another musician unafraid to push at boundaries.

Finally, as someone born on Tyneside, part of an area with a massive regional identity, I feel very at home in Brittany. While Stivell wasn't born there, and spent most of his formative years in Paris, his Breton roots run very deep, and are inseparable from his music. He's an artist I return to from time to time when I feel the need to immerse myself in Keltia (ditto the Chieftains).

Most of the music listed in this book is available on major streaming platforms. Dip your toes in the water and enjoy.

ALAN STIVELL

Alan Stivell was born Alan Cochevelou on I June 1944 in the village of Riom, just north of Clermont-Ferrand in the Auvergne region of France, the son of a civil servant. Cochevelou senior was a Breton and a harp-maker in addition to his government work. He had seized on the idea of recreating the Celtic harp, an instrument commonly in use in mediaeval Brittany, but which had virtually fallen out of use by the 20th century. By the time Alan was nine, his father had built such a harp, based on a fusion of the larger modern concert harp and illustrations in the Brian Boru manuscript. The harp was given to Alan, who was then taught by a combination of his father and the classical harpist Denise Mégevand. He was also a member of the Bleimor Bagad (a pipe band), where he learnt to play both the pipes and the bombarde. He received tuition in Celtic history and mythology, and in Breton. All these elements can be seen in his musical development. By the age of 11, he was giving harp recitals at concerts organised by UNESCO.

In his teens, he moved to Brittany, and began to perform, initially under his given name but later moved to the stage name of Stivell, which means spring or fountain in Breton (a nod to his real name, Cochevelou being a Francophone version of the Breton kozh stivellou, or the old fountains). The name change coincided with his decision to sing as well as play.

In 1968, he signed his first international recording contract with Philips, with his early albums being released on their Fontana label. Despite this, Stivell remained uncertain about how singing in Breton would be received by the wider public; at the time, the use of Breton was frowned upon by the Gaullist government. He was also looking to the idea of a Celtic folk-rock fusion, but his background in the pipe band movement meant he had few, if any, contacts in rock, and was uncertain whether anyone felt the same way. A chance meeting with Breton guitarist Dan Ar Braz kickstarted the rest of his career, as he came in touch with a variety of similarly minded musicians.

His big break was to come when a concert he was giving at Paris's Olympia was chosen for broadcast on French radio. As there were only three state radio channels at the time, this gave him a large captive audience. The critical response was universally positive, and the subsequent album release sold a million and a half copies. It also catapulted him to international attention.

Musically, he remained restless, and subsequent albums reflect this, mixing rock and pure traditional in equal measure. He also continued to explore new ways of creating his music. This culminated in the release of Symphonie Celtique, a fusion of folk, rock, orchestra, and choir which one critic has described as an attempt to do for Breton music what Bartok and Vaughan Williams had done for Hungarian and English folk music (1).

Subsequently, he released music very much on his own terms, exploring different areas, and incorporating them into his core basis of Breton music and culture. Rather like Neil Young, the listener is forced to accept a recording on the artist's terms, rather than for the artist to deliver what they were expecting. This means that, depending on the listener's own likes or degree of open-mindedness, each release can be a disappointment or revelation. What they will get, irrespective of their own feelings, is a work of the utmost integrity.

Throughout the 80's, Stivell remained open to new techniques and influences, seen most clearly in Brian Boru and 1 Douar. The latter album came from a collaboration with Youssou N'Dour, and achieved a remarkable, and successful, fusion of Celtic and African music.

He has subsequently moved back more obviously to Celtic roots, but with increasing influences from global sources. His desire to achieve musical fusions remains undiminished.

In 2012, the 40th anniversary of the Olympia concert was marked by another concert at the same venue. Listening to this reveals a riotous celebration of his musical career.

He has since released another two albums which show him continuing to push musical boundaries and production techniques. In his late seventies, his creative urges seem undiminished.

Perhaps the best thing to do is to finish with the man in his own words. On his website, he describes his musical aims thus:

> *openness to new influences*

*unprecedented blending of different styles of music
continual quest for research and innovation and new technologies
attachment to his cultural roots*

References:
1. Alan Stivell: Bard of Breizh (https://stevewinick.com/stivell)
2. http://www.alanstivell.bzh/en/biography.php

RECORDINGS

HARPE CELTIQUE (TELENN GELTIEK)
(1964 Disques Dreyfus)

Abeir Is Me Huagneach?
A Bhirlinn Bharrach
Plijadur Ha Displijadur
Gwerz Maro Pontkalleg - Barzaz Breiz
Tir-Nan-Og (Chanson De Pêcheur De L'île De Skye)
Na Reubairean (Chanson De Pirate)
Kloareg Trelemo
Una Bhan (Ouna La Blanche)
Kouskit Buan Ma Bihan! (Berceuse)
Mona
Tir Fo Thuinn (Le Pays Qui Est Sous Les Vagues)

REFLETS (REFLECTIONS)
(1970 Fontana)

Reflets
Suites Des Montagnes
Marig Ar Pollanton
Broceliandes
Son Ar Chistr
Sally Free And Easy
Suite Irlandaise
Sil Vestrig
Tenval An Deiz

RENAISSANCE OF THE CELTIC HARP
(1971 Fontana)

Ys
Marv Pontkalleg
Extracts from Penllyn
Manuscripts of Harp Music
Ap Huw
Penllyn
Eliz Eza

Gaeltacht
Caitlin Traill
Port ui Muirgheasa
Airde Cuan
Na Reubairain
Manx Melody
Heman Dubh
Gaelic Waltz
Struan Robertson
The Little Cascade
Braigh Loch Lall
Port an Deorai

À L'OLYMPIA
(1972 Fontana)

The Wind Of Keltia
An Dro
The Trees They Grow High
An Alarc'H
An Durzhunel
Telenn Gwad
The Foggy Dew

Pop Plinn
Tha Mi Sgith
The King Of the Fairies
Tri Martolod
Kost Ar C'Hoad
Suite Sudarmoricaine

Live but featuring only new, previously unreleased tracks

CHEMINS DE TERRE (FROM CELTIC ROOTS)
(1973 Fontana)

Susy Mac Guire
Ian Morrisson Reel
She Moved Through The Fair
Cân Y Melinydd
Oidhche Mhaith
An Dro Nevez

Maro Ma Mestrez
Brezhoneg Raok
An hani A Garan
Metig
Kimiad

E LANGONNED
(1974 Fontana)

E Parrez Langonned
Gavotten Pourled
Planedenn
Ne Bado Ket Atao
Bwthyn Fy Nain
Ffarwel I Aberystwyth
Briste Leathair Pheadair
Mairseal A' Chearc
Dans Fisel
Gavotten Ar Menez

An Sagart Cheolnhar
Bal Fisel
Deus Ganin Me D'Am Bro
Jenovefa
Sagart O Donaill
Diougan Gwenc'hlan
Ar Voraerion
Faili Faili Oro
Oye Vie

E DULENN (À DUBLIN)
(1975 Fontana)

Spered Hollvedel
Delivrance
Ha Kompren't 'vin Erfin
Tenwal E'Or Bred
Digor Eo An Rinceoir
Debhair An Rinceoir

Pachpi Kozh/Pachpi New'
Laridenn/Maieseal O'Neil
Ton Bal-Pouled/Hanter-Drou
Haou
Bal Ha Dans Plinn
An Droiu

Live but featuring only new, previously unreleased tracks

TREMA'N INIS (VERS L'ÎLE)
(1976 Keltia III)

Stok Ouzh an Enez
Hommes Liges des Talus en Transe
Rinnenn XX
An Eur-Se Tost D'ar Peurbad
Negro Song
E-tal ar Groaz
Ar Chas doñz 'Yelo Da Ouez

RAOK DILESTRA: AVANT D'ACCOSTER (BEFORE LANDING)
(1977 Fontana)

Hon anser Dremenet – Our past
The Ancient Celts
Ar Vritonned Ba'inis Breizh
Britons Exile to Armorica
Rouantlallezh Vreizh
Dugelezh Vreizh
The Union Pact
Emsawadagou
The French Revolution and the 19th Century
20th Century Part one

Eil Loden An Ugent Wed
Kantwed

Hon Anser Vreman – Our present
Da Ewan
Marw Ewide E Fobl
Gwariziad Diffinet
Naw Breton 'Ba' Prizon
Tamm-Kreiz New
Plinn

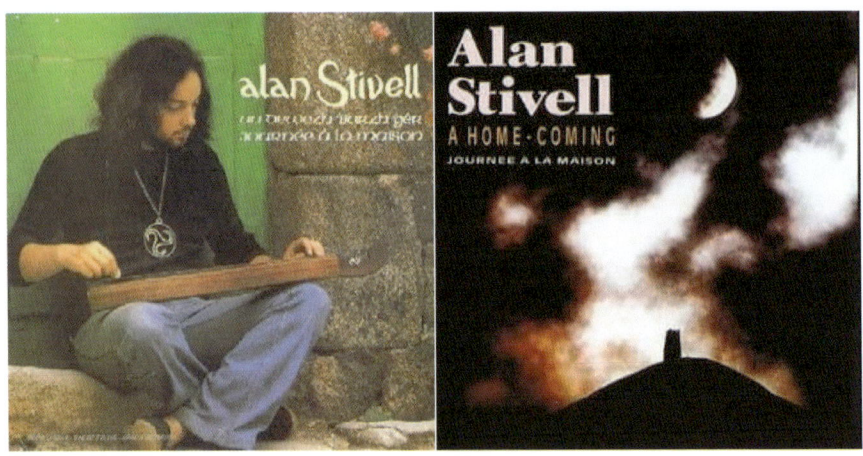

UN DEWEZH 'BARZH 'GER: JOURNEE À LA MAISON
(A HOMECOMING)
(1978 Keltia III)

Trinquons nos Verres
Ar Wezen Awalòu
Henchoú Kuzh
Tabud Kemper
Warlec'h Koan

An Try Marrak
'Tal an Tan
An Nighean Dubh
Sián Chearbheallain
Inisi Henternos

INTERNATIONAL TOUR: TRO AR DED
(1979 CBS/Keltia III)

Ar C'Hoant Dimezin
Rouantelezh Vreizh
Dugelezh Vreizh
Stok Ouzh an Enez
Liegemen of the Trembling Slopes

We Shall Survive
Cailin Og Deas
O' Carolan's Farewell
An Nighean Dubh
Fest-Hypnoz

SYMPHONIE CELTIQUE: TIR NA N OG
(CELTIC SYMPHONY)
(1980 CBS)

Disc one : Kelc'h Unan : Premier Cercle & Kelc'h Duan: Deuxième Cercle

Beaj
Hiraezh: Gwerz 1
Hiraezh: Loc'h Ar Goulenn
Divodan

Emskiant
Kendaskren
Imram
Dilestran

Disc Two : Kelc'h Tri :Troisième Cercle

Ar C'hammou Kentan
Ar Geoded Skedus
Ar Bale Trema'r Geoded
Ar Geoded Skedus (Suite)

Gouel Hollvedel I
Gouel Hollvedel II
Gouel Hollvedel III
Gouel Hollvedel IV
An Distro

TERRE DES VIVANTS: BED AN DUD VEW
(1981 Disc'Az)

Terre Des Vivants
Rentrer En Bretagne
Beg Ar Van
M.J
'Raog Mont D'Ar Skol (Prononcer "Rock Monday School")
Androïdes (1°, 2°, 3° Partie)
Ideas
Androïdes (4° Partie)
Hidden Through The Hills
Cameronian Rant
Q Celts Fiesta
L'Ere Du Verseau

LEGEND (LEGENDE) (MOJENN)
(1983 Disc'Az)

"Si J'Avais 1000 Ans" - Film De Monique Enckell
Tour An Arvor - La Tour D'Armor
Barn – Condamnation
Azenor
Sawen – La Toussaint
Tour en Arvor
"Eireog Shineidin" D'Après Jenny's Chicken Reel
"Immran Brain" – Le Voyage de Bran

La Venue Des Peuples "Dieux" - Teacht Na D'Tuatha Dé Danann
Les Peuples Dieux De Danu - Tuatha Dé Danann
Dagda & Morrigan
Eríu
Dans La Tertre – Sa charme
Le Paloid de Cristal – An Lios Gloine
Le Festin – An Lith
Le Songe D'Angus – Aisling Aengusa
Le Pacte – Comflaithuis
Au-delà Des o Vagues – Dar Noi Tonna

HARPES DU NOUVEL ÂGE (TELENN A' SKUILH DOUR
(1985 Keltia III)

Musique Sacrée
Tremen'R
Pep Tra (1) (Tout Passe)
Pedenn Ewid Breizh (Prière Pour La Bretagne)
Tremen'Ra Pep Tra (2)
Spered Santel (L'Esprit)
Dor I (Porte 1): Musique Expérimentale (Taol-Arnod)
Piberezh: Adaptation De
Piobaireachd (Musique Classique De Cornemuse)
Cumh Chlaibhersm
Lament For The Children
McDonuill Of The Isles
Dor II: Improvisation (Taol-Prim)
Rory Dall's Love Tune (Ou Tabhair Dom Do Lamh)
Kervalan: Court Extrait D'Un Morceau De Ó Carolan (Marbhnagh O'Neill)
Luskellerezh (Berceuse, Balancement)
Dihun' Ta! (Réveille-Toi!) Marche Traditionnelle De Ma Région
En Dro Inis-Arzh (Autour De L'Île D'Arzh)
Dans Fanch Mitt
Suite Écossaise
Dor III: Harp' Noun! (Aide-Moi !)

THE MIST OF AVALON
(1991 Mercury)

La Dame du Lac
Morgan
Camaalot (Hymn I)
Guenievre
Le Chant de Taliesin
La Blessure d'Arthur
Le Val Sans Retour
Belenton

Olwen
Quest
An Advod
Horses on the Hills
Strink Ar Graal
From Awallach
Gaelic Tribes Gathering
The Return (Hymn II)

AGAIN
(1993 Keltia III)

Suite Sudarmoricaine
An Dro / Tha Mi Sgìth
Ar An Garraig / Telenn Wad
The Foggy Dew
Suzy Mc Guire (Siobhan Ni Dhuibhir)
Suite Irlandaise
Spered Hollvedel
Son Ar Chistr
Marv Ma Mestrez

Kimiad
Suite Des Montagnes
Metig
Pop-Plinn
Bal-Ha-Dans-Plinn
O'Neil's March / The King Of The Fairies
Ian Morrisson Reel
Tri Martolod

Studio re-recordings with new arrangements and guest vocalists

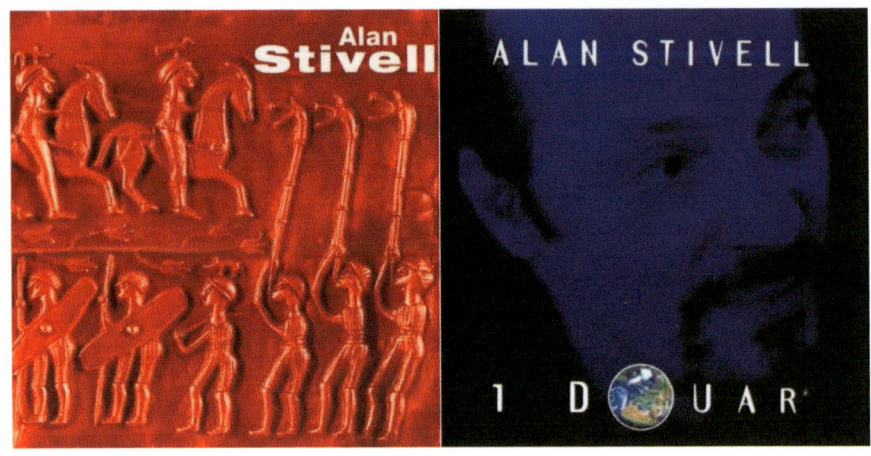

BRIAN BORU
(1995 Keltia III)

Brian Boru	Cease Fire
Let the Plinn	De' Ha Bla'
Mina na Heireann	Sword Dance
Ye Banks and Braes	Parlament Lament
Mairi's Wedding	Lands of My Fathers

1 DOUAR (EUNN DOUAR)
(1998 Disques Dreyfus)

A United Earth 1	Ever
La Mémoire de L'Humain	Kennavo Glenmor
Hope	Una's Love
Ensemble (Understand)	Aet On (Into the Universe's
Crimes	Breath)
A United Earth 2	A United Earth 3
Scots Are Right	

A number of tracks are collaborations with, among others, Youssou N'Dour, Jim Kerr, John Cale and Paddy Moloney

BACK TO BREIZH
(1999 Disques Dreyfus)

Vers Les Iles et Villes de Verre
Rêves (Hunvreoú)
Ceux Qui Sément La Mort
Arvor-You
Rock-Harp
Skoit 'N Tried!

Iroise
E Kreiz Hag Endro
Back to Breizh!
Harpe de Vies
Brian Boru (in French)
Sudarmoricain (Suite)

AU DELÀ DES MOTS
(EN TU-HONT D'AR C'HOMZOU) (BEYOND WORDS)
(2002 Keltia III)

La Harpe, L'Eau, Le Vent
La Celtie et L'Infini (A)
La Celtie et L'Infini (B)
Dihan Telenn V Marzhinn
La Harpe et L'Enfant
Bleimor, La Bagad
Gourin-Pontivy

E Kreiz Breizh
Goltraidhe
Et Les Feuilles Répousseront
Demain Matin Chez O'Carolan
Harpe Atlantique
La Celtie et :l'Infini (C)
La Harpe, L'Eau. Le Vent (B)

EXPLORE
(2006 Keltia III)

Miz Tu	Into
Là-Bas, Là-Bas	Druidic Lands
You Know It (Anao'rit)	Menez
Té (Beyond Words)	Explore
They	Un Parfait Paradis (Miz Tu 2)

EMERALD-EMRODEZ-EMERAUDE
(2009 Kelta III)

Brittany's – Ar Bleizi Mor	Eibhlin – Eileen a Roon
Lusk – Sky Boat Song	Aquarelle – Er Penn All D'al
Marionig	Lenneg
Tamm Ha Tamm – Rennes, Nantes & Brest	Ar Hirañ Noz – Noël, Espoir, Ar Hyd Y Nos
Gael's Call – Gloach Na nGael	Mac Crimon Part I
Harplinn	Mac Crimon Part II
Goadec Rock	Mac Crimon Part III

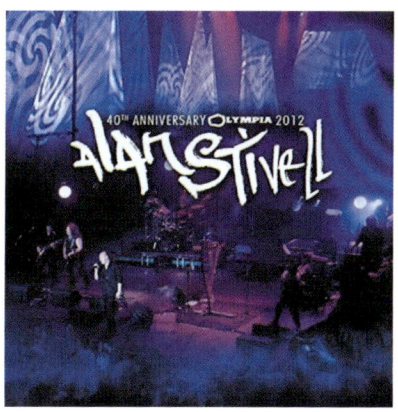

40th ANNIVERSARY OLYMPIA 2012
(2013 Universal Music)

This was a simultaneous CD/DVD release. Track listings are given for both.

CD Version

Présentation
Bleimor, The Bagad
Eibhlin
The Wind of Keltia
Brian Boru
Té
La Hargne Au Coeur (Mo Nighean Donn Nam Meal-shùilean)
Ne Bado Ket Atao
Brittany's
Kimiad
Miz Tu
Suite Sudarmoricaine
Son Ar Christr
Tri Martolod
Bro Gozh (Land of My Fathers – Bro Gozh Fy Nadhau)

DVD Version

Brian Boru – Genérique Instrumental
Bleimor, the Bagad
Eibhlin
O Langonned I
The Wind of Keltia
The Trees They Do Grow High
Iroise
Brian Boru
Té
La Hargne Au Coeur (Mo Nighean Donn Nam Meal-shùilean)
Medley – Telenn Wad, The Foggy Dew
The King of the Fairies
An Alarc'h
Tamm Ha Tamm
Gael's Call
Medley – Jigs (Port an Deorai, Port Ui Mhuirgheasa)
Tamm Kreiz (Pa 'oan O Sevel)
Ne Bado Ket Atao
Brittany's
Kimiad
Miz Tu
An Dro
Tha Mi Sgith
Suite Sudarmoricaine
40 Vloaz 'Zo
Pop Plinn
Son Ar Christr
Ian Morrison Reel
Brezhoneg 'Raok
Tri Martolod
Bro Gozh (Land of My Fathers – Bro Gozh Fy Nadhau)

AMZER: SEASONS
(2015 World Village)

New' Amzer (Spring)
Other Times - Amzeriou All
(Haiku de Printemps)
Matin de Printemps
Mintin New Hanv
Au Plus Pres des Limites
Postscript

Kala Goanv
What Could I Do
Kerzu – December
Purple Moon
Halage
Echu Ar Goanv

HUMAN – KELT
(2018 World Village)

Setu (Audio-Préface/Medley)
Den I (Mɔgɔ)
Den II (Simply Human)
Com Una Gran Orquestra (Ideas)
Ardaigh Cuan
A Hed An Nos (All Through the Night)
BZHg (Self Remix)
Brezhoneg 'Raok
Printemps Automne Autant (As a Haiku)
MJ A Garan (50 Bloaz)
Reflets, Askadoú, Reflections

Bresellen, Brocéliande
Son Ar Christr (My Cheers to You!)
Tri Martolod (New')
Kelti[k]a
Boudicca (Cacos ac Caesar!)
An Englew (La Pacte)
Dor Tir Na nÓg (from Symphonie Celtique)
Éamonn an Cnoic I
Pourquoi Es-Tu Venu Si Tard (Éamonn an Cnoic II)

SINGLES

Crépuscule sur la Rade/ Ballade pour un Matin de Pluie (Fontana 1968)
Flower Power EP (Flower Power/Le Bourreau/Là Oú Va Le Vent/Les Veniteux (Fontana 1968)
Reflet/ Suite Irlandaise (Fontana 1970)
Tha Mi Sgith/ Suite Sudarmoricaine (Fontana 1971, rereleased 1973 with the sides reversed)
Brocéliande/ Son Ar Christr (Chanson à Boire)(Fontana 1971)
Tri Martolod/The King of the Fairies (Fontana 1971)
Eliz Iza/ Port an Deorai (Fontana 1971)
The Wind of Keltia /Pop Plinn (Fontana 1971)
Ian Morrison Reel/Suzy MacGuire (Fontana 1973)
Brezhoneg' Raok/ Metig (Fontana 1973)
Dans Fisel /An Sagart Cheoinhar (Fontana 1974)
Spered Hollvede/ Delivrance (Keltia III 1975)
Digor Eo An Hant/Laridenn/Mairseal O Neil (Keltia III 1975)
Gwiziad Difinnet (Racines Interdit/Naw Breton 'Ba' Prizon (Neuf Bretons en Prison) (Keltia III 1976)
Da Ewan/ Rouantelez Vreizh (Keltia III 1977)
Imram (Lq Queste)/Voyage to the Isle (CBS 1980) – Limited edition promo
'Raog Mont Dar S'kol/ Beg ar Van (extrait) (Disc'Az 1981)
Dans Fach Mitt/ Rory Dall's Love (WEA 1985) – Limited edition promo
Delirium/ Waroak Brest-Armorique (WEA 1987)
Mairi's Wedding (Radio Edit)/ De'Ha Bla' (Disques Dreyfus 1995) – Promo
Let the Plinn (Radio Edit)/ Mnà ha Héireann (Women of Ireland) (Disques Dreyfus 1995)
Brian Boru (Radio Edit/ Cease Fire (Disques Dreyfus 1995)
La Mémoire de L'Humain (Radio Edit)/ Una's Love (Keltia III 1998)
Mintin Sioul/ Stiveloú Kozh (Disques Dreyfus 1998)
Back to Breizh (Disques Dreyfus 2000)
Armoricaine (Suite) (Radio Edit)/Kreiz Hag Endro (Disques Dreyfus 2000)

Rod Ar Vehuz (A)/Orin/Rod Ar Vehuz (B) (Disques Dreyfus 2002) – Promo
Miz Tu (Keltia III 2006) – Promo
Brittany's (Keltia III 2009) – Promo
Lusk – Skye Boat Song (Keltia III 2009) – promo
Tri Martolod/Suite Sudarmoricaine/Brian Boru/Pop Plinn (Live) (Mercury 2011) – Promo Sampler
Bienvenue au Pays de Vilaines Suite Sudarmoricaine/Mairi's Wedding/De' Ha Bla (MPO Disques undated) - Advertising record for the "Communauté de communes de Villaines la Juhel - Mayenne - France"

Alan Stivell and Nolwenn Leroy by Gregor Tanguay

COMPILATIONS

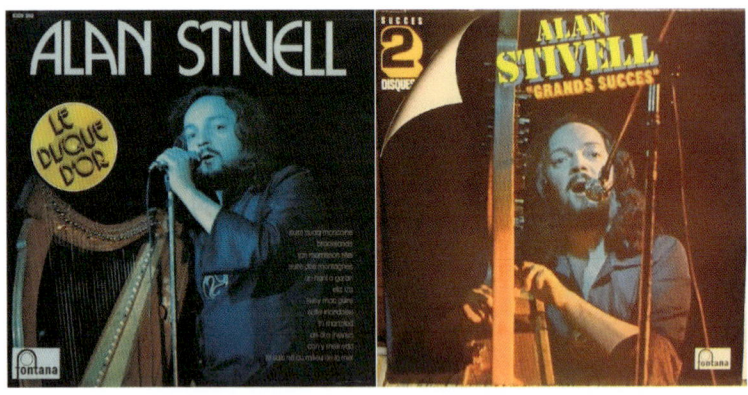

alan stivell
PHILIPS
Reimpression
alan stivell
chante ses plus grands succès de 1970 à 1974

CELTIC ROCK
Alan Stivell
VERTIGO

ATTENTION!
ALAN STIVELL!
fontana
special

alan Stivell
70/95
>ZOOM<

The Best Of
Alan Stivell

Alan Stivell
masterserie

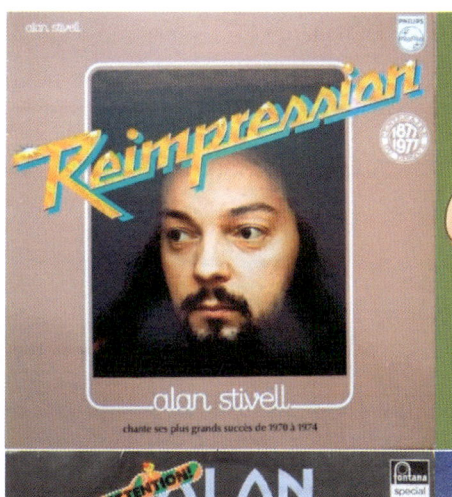

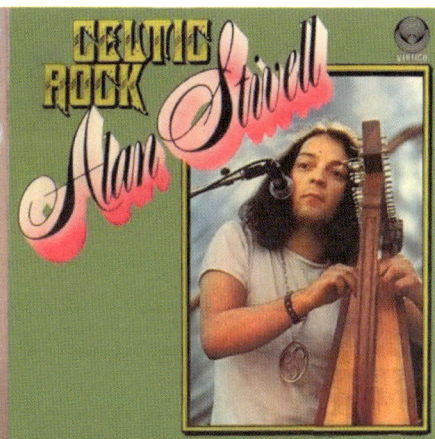

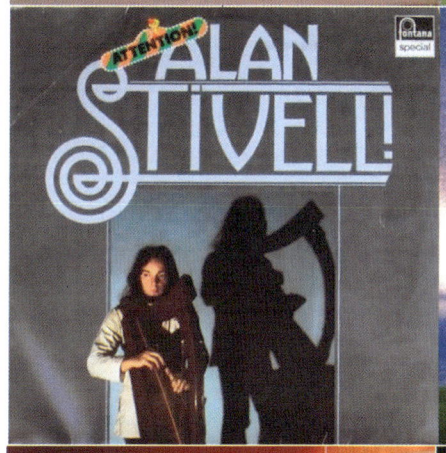

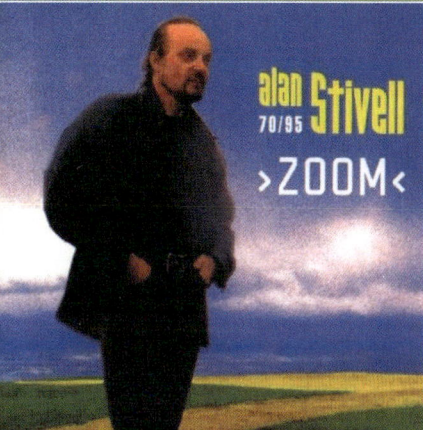

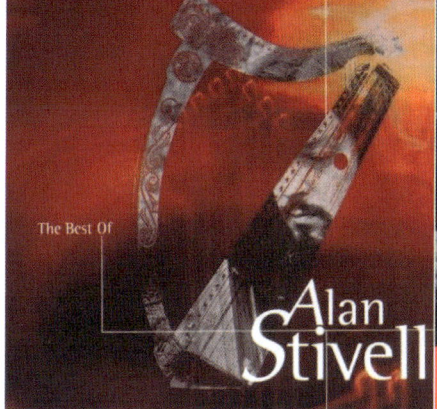

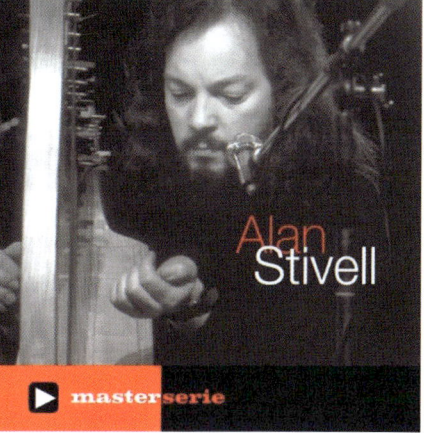

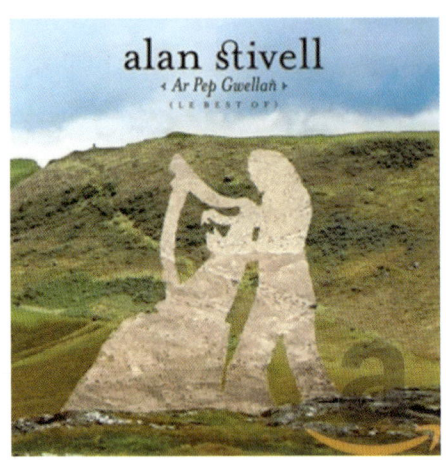

DVDs

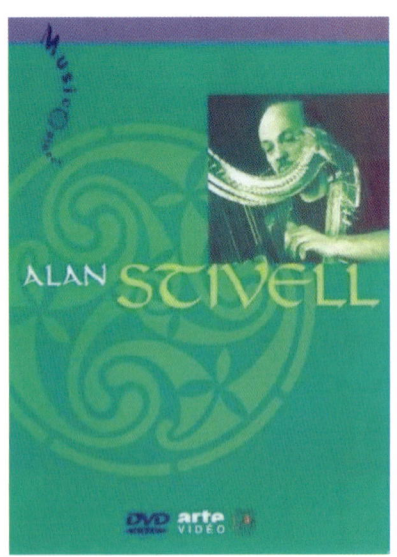

ALAN STIVELL playing Irish Pipes courtesy of Cathy Goubil

ESSENTIAL DISCOGRAPHIES FROM APS BOOKS

(www.andrewsparke.com)

Alan Stivell
Alex Harvey
Alice Cooper
Amon Duul II
Andy White
Blue Nile
Bonzo Dog Band
Can
Caravan
Catherine Howe
Cher
Clifford T. Ward
Colin Blunstone
Culture
Curved Air
Ekseption
Emerson Lake & Palmer
The Enid
Fagans
Fairport Convention
Faust
Focus
Gentle Giant
Gil Scott-Heron
Graham Parker
Ian Hunter
Ijahman
James McMurtry
Jeff Beck
Jess Roden
Jethro Tull
John Lennon
John Martyn
John Stewart
Johnny Clegg
Kate Bush
Kevin Ayers
The Kinks
Led Zeppelin
Leonard Cohen

Linda Ronstadt
Luka Bloom
Madison Violet
Marillion
Meal Ticket
Monkees
Patricia Kaas
Pavlov's Dog
Pink Floyd
Pretenders
Pretty Things
Richard Thompson
Sandy Denny
Show Of Hands
Starry Eyed and Laughing
Steely Dan
Steve Gibbons
Sting
Strawbs
Supertramp
Tom Waits
Tori Amos
Troggs
Warren Zevon
Willie Nile
Wishbone Ash
ZZ Top

Printed in Great Britain
by Amazon